the little book of
HUGS

the little book of
HUGS

Raymond Glynne

ARCTURUS

PICTURE ACKNOWLEDGEMENTS

Ardea: 11, 13, 15, 21, 26, 32, 33, 67, 70, 74, 82, 91, 96.

Corbis: 6, 19, 29, 30, 31, 38, 39, 46, 47, 52, 57, 59, 60, 69, 72, 75, 83, 85, 95.

Creative Image Library: 77.

FLPA: 12, 22, 23, 27, 34, 37, 50, 51, 53, 54, 55, 79, 80, 84, 86.

Getty: 14, 35, 36, 41, 76, 78, 93.

Image Bank: 71.

Nature Picture Library: 8, 16, 18, 24, 25, 43, 45, 63, 65, 87, 88, 89.

PA Photos: 92.

photos.com: 17, 40, 66.

Shutterstock: 7, 9, 10, 20, 28, 42, 44, 48, 49, 56, 58, 61, 62, 68, 73, 81, 90, 94.

Superstock: 64.

ARCTURUS

This edition published in 2011 by Arcturus Publishing Limited
26/27 Bickels Yard, 151–153 Bermondsey Street,
London SE1 3HA

Copyright © 2010 Arcturus Publishing Limited

ISBN: 978-1-84837-759-2
AD001671EN

Printed in China

Arms have many uses, too numerous to list here, but surely the best use they can be put to is to hold someone you care about. A hug can convey a vast range of emotions: love or remorse, happiness or sorrow, pride or sympathy, fear or relief – whatever we're feeling, it helps to share it and the only way to do that is with a hug.

It's a gesture so powerful that it doesn't need words. So make someone's day and say it with a hug.

Hugging is a natural instinct for us all...

It's the most comfortable sleeping position…

The need for a hug will drive us to great lengths...

Some of us will hug anything...

Or nothing…

We claim our loved ones with a hug...

To let the world know they're ours…

It's a bonding gesture…

A need for reassurance …

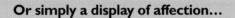

Or simply a display of affection…

IT'S BETTER WHEN WE'RE TOGETHER

Hugs are for happy reunions…

For breaking the ice...

A hug shows how much you've missed them…

Or how much you're going to miss them...

And how much you want them to stay…

A hug says you're on the same side…

You're one of the gang...

It's a display of solidarity…

A reassuring gesture…

After all, two heads are better than one…

A hug is our way of protecting the young…

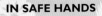

Keeping them where we can see them…

Some need protecting from the outside world…

Others just need protecting from themselves…

And sometimes we all need protecting…

Life can be pretty hair-raising at times...

A hug can inspire courage...

It confirms you're not going it alone…

Sometimes you need someone to hide behind…

Or hide with…

We share one another's joy with a hug...

It strengthens our team spirit…

Makes us laugh…

Helps us to bond...

And find sheer happiness...

When things don't go your way, a hug can help...

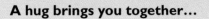

A hug brings you together…

It can bring you back into the fold...

Soothe an aching heart…

A hug can make everything right...

Hugs can shield you from the big wide world...

Sometimes you just have to cling on...

Let someone else take the strain…

Just go along for the ride…

And share in the pride of a job well done...

It can get pretty cold out there...

Sometimes we all need a team huddle...

A hug can be a real heartwarmer...

Of course, some are more eager than others…

But a bit of shared warmth is always welcome...

The best hugs are spontaneous…

The impulse to hug is strong...

It can catch you off guard…

Or come completely out of the blue…

But a little caution is advisable at times...

Some hugs are launched on the unsuspecting…

They can turn into a wrestling match...

Or a game of rough and tumble...

Where only one comes out on top...

But everyone comes up smiling…

Hugging's so easy you can do it in your sleep...

It's a natural resting position...

You don't need pillows when you've got hugs…

Of course, some spend more time doing it than others...

And it can be a little uncomfortable…

A hug expresses the love that knows no boundaries…

The joy of being together...

That up-close-and-personal feeling…

Even when the logistics are tricky...

A hug is a knot that binds you...

Friends never hold back...

From showing their affection...

They hug when they meet...

While they're watching the game...

And when they part...

Some hugs require a little exertion…

But they're worth all the effort...

They can really bring you out of your shell...

They can make you feel on top of the world...

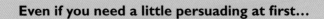

Even if you need a little persuading at first…

When you've fallen out...

And sorry seems to be the hardest word…

There's only one thing to do…

Hugging reunites us…

And makes us forget our differences...

Hugs help you find your soulmate…

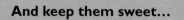

And keep them sweet…

You can be like two peas in a pod...

Or a bit of a mismatch...

All that matters is that you've got each other…